BLIZZARD

by Joyce Markovics

Consultant:
Daphne Thompson, Meteorologist
Educational Outreach Coordinator
Cooperative Institute for Mesoscale Meteorological Studies
National Weather Center

BEARPORT
PUBLISHING

New York, New York

Credits
Cover, © iStockphoto/Thinkstock; 4–5, © Don Landwehrle/Alamy; 6–7, © Stock Connection Blue/Alamy; 8–9, © Dainis Derics/Shutterstock; 10–11, © Scott Olson/Getty Images; 12–13, © John Churchman/Getty Images; 14–15, © PCJones/Alamy; 15, © The Power of Forever Photography; 16–17, © Frances Roberts/Alamy; 18–19, © Levranii/Shutterstock; 20–21, © Noel Hendrickson/Getty Images; 22, © Jason Lindsey/Alamy; 23TL, © Don Landwehrle/Alamy; 23TR, © The Power of Forever Photography; 23BL, © Frances Roberts/Alamy; 23BR, © Alex Wong/Getty Images.

Publisher: Kenn Goin
Senior Editor: Joyce Tavolacci
Creative Director: Spencer Brinker
Design: Debrah Kaiser
Photo Researcher: Picture Perfect Professionals, LLC

Library of Congress Cataloging-in-Publication Data in process at time of publication (2014)
Library of Congress Control Number: 2013032743
ISBN-13: 978-1-62724-125-0 (library binding)

For more information, write to Bearport Publishing Company, Inc., 45 West 21st Street, Suite 3B, New York, New York 10010. Printed in the United States of America.

10 9 8 7 6 5 4 3 2 1

CONTENTS

BLIZZARDS

Snowflakes fall from the sky.

Soon, strong winds begin to blow.

A **blizzard** is coming!

Snow is made up
of tiny bits of ice.

5

During a blizzard, winds blow 35 miles per hour (56 kph) or more.

Swoosh!

Wind blows the snow all around.

The swirling snow makes it hard to see.

7

A blizzard is a bad winter storm.

It can bring heavy snow and high winds.

8

A **whiteout** is when blowing snow makes it hard to see.

A blizzard makes roads icy and snowy.

Cars slide on the ice.

They get stuck in the snow.

Blizzards can bring several feet of snow.

Heavy snow blocks doorways.

Then people may get trapped in buildings.

Winds from a blizzard often blow snow into huge piles. The piles are called snowdrifts.

Sometimes, people get caught outside in a blizzard.

They can get lost in the blowing snow.

When parts of a person's body get very cold, they can freeze. This is called **frostbite**.

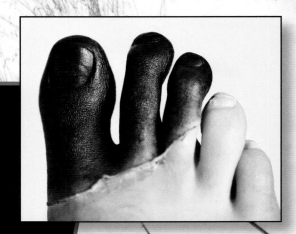

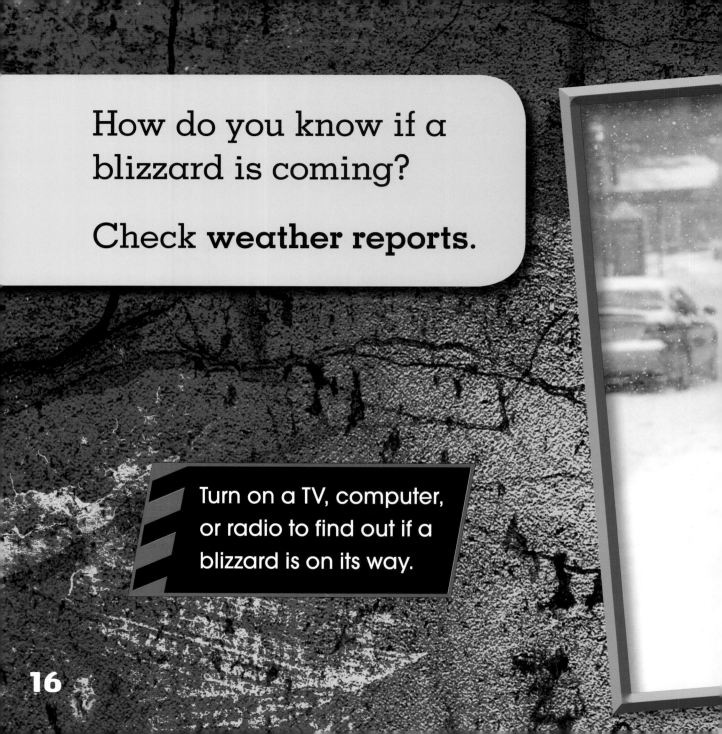

How do you know if a
blizzard is coming?

Check **weather reports**.

Turn on a TV, computer,
or radio to find out if a
blizzard is on its way.

Stay indoors during a blizzard.

This is the best way to keep safe and warm.

It is not safe to travel during a blizzard.

Be ready if the heater in your home stops working.

Have warm clothes and blankets nearby.

Protect yourself from a blizzard's icy blast!

Blizzards can last for hours or even days.

BLIZZARD FACTS

- Most blizzards occur in the United States, Canada, and Russia.

- A blizzard can have temperatures as low as 10°F (–12°C)—or even lower.

- A blizzard's blowing snow stops people from seeing more than a quarter mile (0.4 km) in front of them.

- If you are caught outside during a blizzard, find shelter right away.

- Make sure your family has a flashlight in case the power in your home goes out. Also, make sure your family has a radio with batteries so that you can hear weather reports.

blizzard (BLIZ-urd)
a storm with strong
winds and blowing snow

frostbite (FRAWST-*bite*)
damage to part of the body
due to extreme cold

weather reports
(WETH-ur rih-PORTS)
reports that tell what the
weather will be like in the
coming hours or days

whiteout (WITE-out)
a weather condition in
which blowing snow
makes it hard to see far

INDEX

READ MORE

Bullard, Lisa. *Blizzards (Pull Ahead Books)*. Minneapolis, MN: Lerner (2009).

Goin, Miriam Busch. *Storms (Science Readers)*. Washington, DC: National Geographic (2009).

LEARN MORE ONLINE

To learn more about blizzards, visit
www.bearportpublishing.com/ItsaDisaster!

ABOUT THE AUTHOR

Joyce Markovics lives along the Hudson River in Tarrytown, New York. She enjoys sipping steamy mugs of hot cocoa and riding horses in the snow.